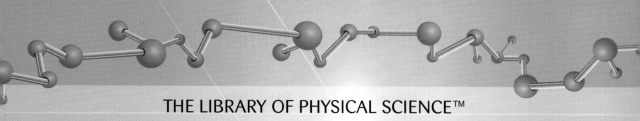

THE LIBRARY OF PHYSICAL SCIENCE™

The Properties of Gases

Marylou Morano Kjelle

The Rosen Publishing Group's

PowerKids Press™

New York

For my nephews, Kyle James and Ryan Trevor Hogan

Published in 2007 by The Rosen Publishing Group, Inc.
29 East 21st Street, New York, NY 10010

First Edition

Editors: Daryl Heller, Joanne Randolph, Suzanne Slade
Book Design: Elana Davidian
Photo Researcher: Marty Levick

Photo Credits: Cover, p. 9 © Spencer Grant/Photo Edit; p. 4 Russell Kightley/Photo Researchers, Inc.; pp. 6, 13, 21 © Royalty-Free/Corbis; p. 7 Adam Hart-Davis/Photo Researchers, Inc.; p. 8 © Dana White/Photo Edit; p. 10 © C Squared Studios/Photodisc Green/Getty Images; p. 11 Alexis Rosenfeld/Photo Researchers, Inc.; p. 12 Educational Images, Ltd/Custom Medical Stock Photo; p. 14 © David Young-Wolff/Photo Edit; p. 15 © Heinrich van den Berg/Gallo Images/Getty Images; p. 16 Andrew Lambert Photography/Photo Researchers, Inc.; p. 17 Gusto/Photo Researchers; p. 18 © Frans Lanting/Corbis; p. 19 NASA-KSC; p. 20 © STScI/NASA/Corbis.

Library of Congress Cataloging-in-Publication Data

Kjelle, Marylou Morano.
  The properties of gases / Marylou Morano Kjelle.— 1st ed.
    p. cm. — (The library of physical science)
  Includes index.
  ISBN 1-4042-3423-3 (library binding) — ISBN 1-4042-2170-0 (pbk.) — ISBN 1-4042-2360-6 (six pack)
  1. Gases—Juvenile literature. I. Title. II. Series.

QC161.2.K54 2007
530.4'3—dc22

                                                        2005029484

Manufactured in the United States of America

Contents

Matter on the Move

What do a toad, the air you breathe, and a glass of milk have in common? They are all made of matter. Matter exists in three states. These are solids, liquids, and gases. You cannot always see, smell, or feel gases. However, gases are all around you. All matter, including gases, is made of tiny pieces called molecules. Molecules are made up of one or more **atoms**. A molecule of **oxygen** gas, for example, is made of two oxygen atoms.

Gases have many special **properties** that help us

Molecules of methane gas, shown here, are formed by one carbon atom and four hydrogen atoms. Methane gas in the air helps trap the heat of the Sun.

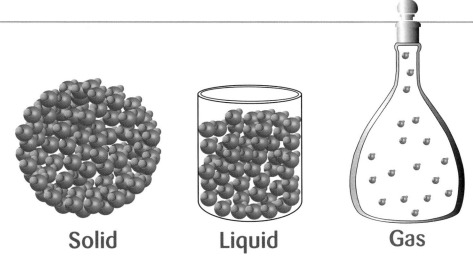

Solid   **Liquid**   **Gas**

The molecules in a solid, liquid, and gas are arranged differently. The molecules in a solid are close together and have a fixed pattern. Liquid molecules have more space between them, and their pattern is looser. Gases have the most space between their molecules, and they do not have a set pattern.

recognize them as gases. Gas molecules are always moving. As gas molecules move, they **bounce** off each other and objects around them. This movement does not change the gas molecule. The gas molecule does not slow down or stick to other gas molecules or to objects. A gas molecule just keeps on moving.

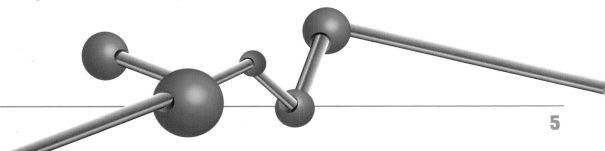

Gases and Fluidity

Bonds, or intermolecular forces, hold together the molecules that make up matter. Molecules that are close together have strong intermolecular forces. For example, the

The air around Earth is filled with gases. This blanket of gases is called the atmosphere.

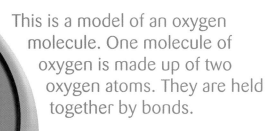

molecules in a solid are packed tightly together. They do not move very much.

Molecules that are far apart have weak intermolecular forces. The molecules in a gas have a lot of space between them.

Gas molecules are small and move quickly. As gas molecules move and bounce off each other, they spread out and fill whatever **container** they are placed in. In fact gases will spread out as far as they can. The movement of molecules is called fluidity. Fluidity allows something to flow.

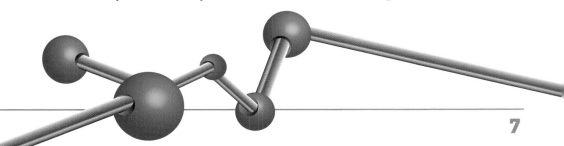

Gases and Volume

The amount of space that a **substance** takes up is called its volume. Gases do not have a set volume. Molecules in a gas move and fill up the volume of the container in which they are placed. If a gas in a small container is put into a larger container, the gas molecules will spread out. They will have greater space between them as they fill the larger volume. For example, suppose you bought a balloon filled with helium gas at the circus. The helium molecules inside the balloon are moving quickly. They are bouncing off each other and

This glass tube is filled with air. If the tube had a lid, the gas would spread out and completely fill the container. Because the tube is open, the gas fills the container and spreads out to fill the surrounding space, too.

These balloons are filled with helium. The helium takes on the shape of the balloon that it fills. If the helium were moved from a small balloon into a larger balloon, it would spread out to fill the new space. Helium is a light gas. It allows the balloons to float in the air.

the sides of the balloon. If you pop the balloon in your bedroom, the helium molecules will move and spread out into your whole room. Soon they will be bouncing off the walls as they fill the entire volume of the room. The helium molecules will be farther apart in your room than they were inside the smaller balloon.

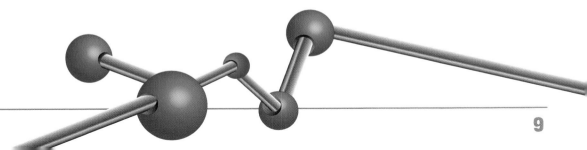

Gases and Shape

The arrangement of molecules gives matter its shape. For example, the shape of a solid is created by the pattern of its tightly packed molecules. The molecules of a gas are not arranged in a pattern. Therefore gas has no shape of its own. Instead it moves to take the shape of whatever is holding it.

For example, there are metal tanks that hold oxygen gas for people to breathe when they swim underwater for a long time. They are shaped like a **cylinder**. The oxygen gas in these tanks moves around and forms the same cylinder shape as the tank. When you blow air into a round

This beach ball is filled with air. If you open the stopper on the ball and push the air out, that air will no longer hold the round shape of the ball.

People need air to breathe. There is no air underwater. However, because gases will fill whatever container they are placed in, we can bring air with us underwater. These people have air tanks on their backs. This lets them breathe as they study the living things and their surroundings in the ocean.

beach ball, the air takes on a round shape, too. The shape of the gas inside each object is the same shape as the object itself.

If the object holding a gas changes shape, the gas inside it also changes shape. For example, suppose you pull on the ends of a round, fat balloon to make it a long, thin balloon. Then the gas inside the balloon will change shape, too.

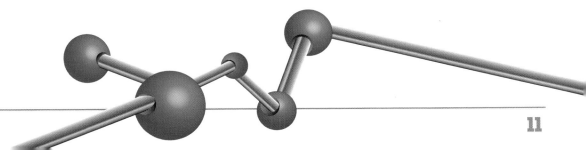

Gases and Expansion

As gas molecules move farther and farther apart, the gas expands, or takes up more volume. Over time a gas will completely fill the space it is in. If the gas is in a closed container, the molecules expand until they are stopped by the walls of the container. If the gas is in an open container, the gas molecules expand out of the container and become part of the air surrounding them.

The movement of gas molecules from one area to another is called diffusion. One way we **experience** diffusion is with our sense of smell. If a bottle

This glass tube has a gas called bromine in it. Because bromine has a color, you can see diffusion in action.

of perfume is opened at one end of a room, in time the scent will be smelled on the other side of the room. The room has become the gas's container. The perfume molecules have mixed with the room's air molecules and have diffused throughout the room.

Natural gas is found in the soil after living things break down under pressure. This gas is used as a fuel for such things as heating our homes and cooking food. Natural gas has no smell, color, or taste. However, people add a smell to natural gas so we will know when it is spreading out, or diffusing, into the air.

Gases and Compressibility

If a gas is forced into a smaller container, the gas will compress, or become smaller. With less room in which to move, the gas molecules are forced closer together. They **squeeze** into the empty spaces that once existed between them.

You compress gas when you pump your bike tires with air. As air is forced into the tire, many gas molecules are squeezed into the tire's small space.

A bike tire is filled with compressed air. The more air you pump into the tire, the firmer the tire becomes. If you put only a little air into the tire, the air would spread out to fill the tire, but the tire would be too soft to use.

Aerosol cans work because a liquid and a gas are compressed inside the can. When the button on top of the can is pressed, it opens a small hole. The gas inside the can expands and moves out of the can. This forces the liquid out in a fine mist.

A gas will stay compressed as long as it stays in a small container. If the container gets bigger, the gas molecules begin to move apart, and the gas expands. Have you ever heard a whooshing sound when you opened a can of soda? That sound is made by a gas called carbon dioxide. It is compressed inside soda cans and makes that noise when it expands.

Density and Temperature

Density is a measure of the amount of matter in a certain volume. Density tells you how closely packed the molecules in a substance are. The closer the molecules of a substance are to each other, the greater its density. The molecules of gases are usually loosely packed, with empty spaces between them. Gases are usually less dense than solids and liquids.

Changing **temperatures** can change how molecules move in a gas. At high temperatures the gas molecules move faster and

Weather is created when temperatures go up or down and the gases in the air crash into each other with greater or lesser force. This causes high-pressure or low-pressure areas. We use a tool called a barometer, shown here, to measure air pressure.

Dry ice does not melt into a liquid. Instead it changes directly into carbon dioxide gas, which sinks toward the ground. The gas sinks because the carbon dioxide gas is denser than the air.

spread farther apart. This increases the gas's volume. Lowering the temperature of a gas slows the molecules down and moves them closer together. The volume of a gas becomes smaller in colder temperatures.

When gas molecules collide, **pressure** is created. Increasing the temperature of a gas will increase its pressure. The molecules will collide with one another and the sides of their container with greater force. Lowering the temperature of a gas lowers its pressure because the gas molecules slow down.

Important Oxygen

Do you know which gas people, animals, and all living things need to live? The answer is oxygen. This gas is colorless, tasteless, and odorless. Oxygen makes up almost 21 **percent** of Earth's **atmosphere**. Trees, bushes, grasses, and other plants create most of Earth's oxygen during **photosynthesis**. During photosynthesis, plants take in a gas called carbon dioxide through their leaves. Plants use the carbon dioxide, sunshine, and

A rain forest is a large, wet area filled with plants and animals. Rain forests once covered 14 percent of Earth. Today they cover only about 7 percent of Earth. Because rain forests are being cut down, we are losing many of the plants that produce the oxygen we need to live.

water to make their food and oxygen gas.

People and animals take in oxygen when they breathe. Once oxygen is inside the body, the blood then carries it to every cell in the body. The body uses the oxygen to make **energy**.

Oxygen is a part of most solids. Solid oxygen makes up about 46 percent of Earth's **crust**. Oxygen gas can also be made into a liquid. Liquid oxygen is added to some **fuels** because it helps the fuel burn faster. This makes liquid oxygen useful in rocket fuel. Rocket fuel is used in the engines of spacecraft, such as the space shuttle. They need a huge amount of energy to blast off.

The space shuttle uses fuel that includes liquid oxygen and hydrogen. This fuel gives the shuttle the power it needs to exit Earth's atmosphere and enter space.

Nitrogen and Hydrogen

Gases other than oxygen are needed for life on Earth. Nitrogen gas makes up about 78 percent of the air around you. Nitrogen gas has no color, odor, or taste. It is nonflammable, which means that it will not burn. Nitrogen gas does not usually combine with other gases or elements.

Hydrogen is the most plentiful gas in the universe. The universe is all of space. Hydrogen is the lightest known gas. Hydrogen has no color, no odor, and no taste. It is flammable, which means that hydrogen burns easily. Hydrogen is almost never

The universe is filled with gases, including hydrogen. The Sun's atmosphere is made mostly of hydrogen.

found alone as a gas. Instead it combines with other elements to form **compounds**.

Did you know that hydrogen combines with another gas to make water? Water is a liquid made from oxygen and hydrogen. Water is quite an important substance. It covers around three-quarters of Earth's surface. All living things depend on it to live. Next time you are swimming, you can think about the gases that made it possible!

Hydrogen combined with carbon can create a compound known as propane. Propane is used in many gas grills. Summer barbecues would not be the same without hydrogen gas!

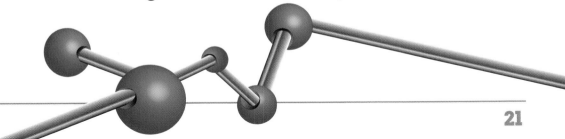

Gases Are Everywhere

A large blanket made of gases surrounds Earth. This blanket of gases is called the atmosphere. The atmosphere reaches hundreds of miles (km) above Earth. In addition to oxygen and nitrogen, gases such as argon, methane, and carbon dioxide are found in Earth's atmosphere. Water vapor, the gaseous form of water, is also in our atmosphere. The gases in our atmosphere keep Earth safe from the harmful rays of the Sun. At the same time, the gases also prevent Earth from getting too cold. They trap the warmth of the Sun's rays that have reached Earth. Without gases we could not breathe. We also would not have the important compounds, such as water, on which we depend.

We cannot see them, feel them, or smell them, but gases surround us. We depend on gases and their properties every day. Our world would not be the same without them.

Glossary

atmosphere (AT-muh-sfeer) The gases around an object in space. On Earth this is air.

atoms (A-temz) The smallest parts of elements that can exist either alone or with other elements.

bounce (BOWNS) To spring up, down, or to the side.

compounds (KOM-powndz) Two or more things combined.

container (kun-TAY-ner) Something that holds things.

crust (KRUST) The outer, or top, layer of a planet.

cylinder (SIH-len-der) A tubelike object.

energy (EH-nur-jee) The power to work or to act.

experience (ik-SPEER-ee-ents) To learn by taking part or seeing for oneself.

fuels (FYOOLZ) Things used to make energy, warmth, or power.

oxygen (OK-sih-jen) A gas that has no color, taste, or odor and is necessary for people and animals to breathe.

percent (pur-SENT) One part of 100.

photosynthesis (foh-toh-SIN-thuh-sus) The way in which green plants make their own food from sunlight, water, and a gas called carbon dioxide.

pressure (PREH-shur) A force that pushes on something.

properties (PRAH-pur-teez) Features that belong to something.

squeeze (SKWEEZ) To crowd into a limited area.

substance (SUB-stans) Matter that takes up space.

temperatures (TEM-pur-cherz) How hot or cold things are.

Index

Web Sites

Due to the changing nature of Internet links, PowerKids
Press has developed an online list of Web sites related
to the subject of this book. This site is updated regularly.
Please use this link to access the list:
www.powerkidslinks.com/lops/gases/